Daniel in the Lions' Den

Contributing Writer
Marlene Targ Brill

Consultant
David M. Howard, Jr., Ph.D.

Illustrations
Thomas Gianni

Publications International, Ltd.

Long ago in the city of Jerusalem, there lived a boy named Daniel. In those days, Jerusalem was ruled by a king named Nebuchadnezzar. The king ordered his soldiers, "Bring all the best royal and noble sons of Jerusalem to my palace in Babylon." The king wanted to train these boys to work in his court.

Daniel was one of the boys chosen by the soldiers. This is how he came to live in Babylon.

At Nebuchadnezzar's palace, the boys were well taught and cared for. Daniel learned more than anyone else. God watched over him and gave him wisdom beyond his years. God gave Daniel the special gift of understanding dreams.

Daniel became known as someone who had the spirit of God in him. He explained what no other person could explain. He served Nebuchadnezzar and every king after him.

Years later, another king by the name of Belshazzar had a party. During the party, a huge hand appeared and made strange writing on the wall.

Daniel explained the writing to the king, "You rebelled against the Lord of Heaven. You worshiped other gods. You thought they were better than He is." The king thanked Daniel and gave him an important job in the kingdom.

The next king, named Darius, planned to give Daniel an even more important job. This made some of the other workers angry.

These other men tried to find a way to make Daniel look bad, but he had done nothing wrong. They decided to trick the king.

They told the king, "We think you should make a law that for the next thirty days people can only pray to you. If they pray to anyone else, they will be thrown to the lions."

The king thought this was a good idea. So he signed the paper to make the law.

Daniel heard about the law, but he continued to pray to God. The evil men saw him praying. They ran back to King Darius and asked, "Didn't you sign a law that said no person should pray to anyone except you?"

The king answered that anyone who broke this law would be thrown into the lions' den.

"Daniel continues to pray to God," the men reported. "He must be punished as you said."

King Darius was shocked. He had never meant to hurt Daniel. He tried to save Daniel. But a law signed by the king could not be changed, not even by the king himself.

Before Daniel was thrown into the den of lions, Darius said to him, "May your God keep you safe."

The king put his royal clay stamp on the rock that covered the entrance to the den. That way he would know that no one had tried to let Daniel out.

King Darius was so sad. He could not eat or sleep. All night long he thought of poor Daniel. He went outside early the next morning and ran to the den. "Daniel," he called out, "Are you alive?"

"Yes, king," answered Daniel, "God sent an angel to shut the mouths of the lions. I have not been harmed."

The king was so happy! God had saved Daniel!

King Darius could not wait to see Daniel. He just had to see for himself that Daniel was not harmed. The king ordered his guards to take Daniel out of the lions' den. Many men came to remove the stone from the opening. The royal seal was still there. They lifted Daniel out of the den.

King Darius greeted Daniel warmly. "I'm so glad you are not harmed," said the king. "Your God protected you."

King Darius ordered his guards to bring the evil men who had tried to have Daniel killed. He decided that they should have the very same punishment they tricked him into giving Daniel.

Then the king wrote to all people throughout his empire: "All the people in my kingdom should obey Daniel's God. This is the God who lives forever. This God saved Daniel from the lions."

From that day on, Daniel lived in peace in the kingdom of Darius.